Instrumentation and Control Made Easy

Volume 9

Maritime 4.0
The Future of Seafaring

To
The Futurists
Of Our Global Maritime Industry

Instrumentation and Control Made Easy

Volume 9

Maritime 4.0
The Future of Seafaring

Elstan A. Fernandez
Cdr Dr. Bhaskar Bhandarkar

SHROFF PUBLISHERS & DISTRIBUTORS PVT. LTD.
Mumbai Bangalore Kolkata New Delhi

Instrumentation and Control Made Easy

Volume 9: Maritime 4.0 - The Future of Seafaring

By *Elstan A. Fernandez and Cdr Dr. Bhaskar Bhandarkar*

First Edition: November 2023

Print ISBN: 978-93-5542-041-1

E_Book ISBN: 978-93-5542-089-3

Published by **Shroff Publishers and Distributors Pvt. Ltd.** B-103, Railway Commercial Complex, Sector 3, Sanpada (E), Navi Mumbai 400705
TEL: (91 22) 4158 4158 • FAX: (91 22) 4158 4141
E-mail : spdorders@shroffpublishers.com • Web : www.shroffpublishers.com
Printed at SAP Print Solutions Pvt. Ltd., Mumbai

Preface to the First Edition

This pocketbook is a primer to help understand the basic nuances of Maritime 4.0 on commercial ships. This is the base on which future ships shall operate and hence will serve as a window to the future of seafaring.

Electro Technical Officers and Marine Engineers onboard commercial ships and those undergoing training to qualify for these positions, will find this book useful.

The Pocket Book Series was introduced because there is a changing trend in the way books are read today. The new normal is that readers and students prefer to read specific, and not so voluminous content, in the least time, as time comes at a premium these days.

Hopefully our team of authors will be able to cater to numerous topics from many relevant subjects.

Any feedback is always welcome!

Elstan A. Fernandez

Acknowledgement

The opportunity to share our acquired knowledge with thousands of professionals and students across many countries and organisations has given us an immense sense of accomplishment and satisfaction. It has also been a wonderful journey of discovery for us - both while researching for this book and teaching the subject in India and abroad.

This book is the result of over 40 years of learning and hands-on experience, including research and collaboration with various organisations and specialists in the global maritime industry.

We sincerely thank all the wonderful people who have supported us in every way, ever since we embarked on this project.

We are indebted to many distinguished persons who have have not only supported our endeavours but also permitted us to publish very valuable content for education. These articles are relevant to the building, safe operation and conscientious survey of commercial ships. Many world-class organisations and manufacturers have extended their invaluable support too. We are grateful for the updated information from their websites and related literature. These inclusions have undoubtedly enriched the content.

Numerous students now realize their dream of being educated through a scholarship program that is funded by the royalty that we receive.

The encouragement from lay people and professionals alike has thus been a stimulus to our enthusiasm. In order to give back and say "thank you" to the maritime fraternity, a free educational website – www.marineelectricity.com is available.

In this context, we have a beautiful quote to share with my readers:

"Real knowledge, like everything else of value, is not to be obtained easily.

It must be worked for, studied for, thought for, and, more than all must be prayed for."

Thomas Arnold (1795-1842), British Educator, Scholar

Elstan's® Pocket Book Series

⚓ Contents ⚓

Prologue

Most of us didn't meet or experience 4.0 by accident; we were destined to be where we are and be part of a tribe that strives to make this world a better place! As I remember, my generation was born at the end of the 2nd Industrial Revolution in a country that was 15 years into independence, with much of the technology belonging to the 1st Industrial Revolution and well, maybe before that too!

In short, we are probably a most blessed generation that has seen the most change and the most progress in our country and in the world at large. So, here's why!

Yes! It has been a roller coaster ride through the world of technology and a tumultuous experience at times but all the same a fruitful one!

Fortunately, some of us were born into families that were and are technologically sound, futurists, part time inventors, curious engineers, designers, ingenious, skilled, shop floor workers, and now we live, breathe, dream, and earn our livelihood through technology.

At about the age of 4 - as I can remember, one of my first favourite toys was a set of wooden tools. My best friends besides dad and mom, were my maternal grandparents - both World War II veterans who enthralled me stories of the First and Second World Wars. Grandpa was a sharpshooter and a Lewis gunner. *The Lewis gun (or Lewis automatic machine gun or Lewis automatic rifle) is a First World War-era light machine gun of US design that was perfected and mass-produced in the United Kingdom and widely used by troops of the British Empire during the war. It had a distinctive barrel cooling shroud (containing a finned, aluminium breech-to-muzzle heat sink to cool the gun barrel) and top-mounted pan magazine).* A devout person, he never killed a man! On the other hand, he had an overflowing trunk of trophies from various musketry championships.

In his childhood, grandpa had a wooden cycle and grew up to own a Harley Davidson motorcycle, and later a motor car; now that is some progress! After the end of the war, he worked in the "Loco Shed" as he called it – a huge workshop in those times, for steam engines (locomotives that were used by the railway). He knew the steam engine through and through. His fascination for steam engines came from seeing his father – a World War I veteran who later took up a job as an engine driver or "engineer" in those days as they were known.

Prologue

Well, most veterans moved to factories and the railways as it was the only means of livelihood. Listening to him and later going for visits to the yard not far away from home and just beside my first school, I learned all about the steam engine. I also learned that this was not only used to pull trains but also as a prime mover for huge machines in factories and power looms too!

Coimbatore, the Manchester of South India, had numerous textile mills. As more and more textile factories mushroomed, he moved to the "mills" as they were now considered experts who could keep the steam-powered looms running. Electricity was almost unheard of in his time and followed through to the days of my father. They used oil lamps at home and wood fires kept the kitchens going. Steam was thus the answer in large factories!

I remember studying in the seventh grade, about William Caxton (c. 1422 – c. 1491) who was an English merchant, diplomat, and writer. He is thought to be the first person to introduce a hand-operated printing press into England, in 1476, and as a printer was the first English retailer of printed books. But here I was hearing about boilers and steam engines. My uncle who worked in the Royal Indian Navy during India's pre-independence era, told us stories of wood-fired boilers and stokers who were experts at stacking and feeding wood into the huge boilers of steam ships. Then came the coal fired ones.

Little did I know it was the second Industrial Revolution! India, till the early 80s, used steam locomotives for trains and that was my means of transport to and from school too! As the world's economies struggled to grow stronger, India too was slowly but surely growing from strength to strength.

And so, I grew up in a mish mash of a technological world. Oldtimers swore by steam and mechanical power while the younger generation that my father belonged to, praised electricity.

Hydraulics wasn't much heard of. By then, my father, the youngest in a family of 8 had his eldest brother, (an inventor and full-time maker of things that were yet unknown to many), motivating him to move into the modern textile and engineering industry. He started out at as a teenager.

In about a decade, he became a sought-after person who erected and managed spinning machines with up to 440 spindles and that were 110 feet long. This was mass production at its best in the city and the textile industry boomed.

Prologue

He soon adapted to and transitioned to electrically operated machines. This breed of self-made engineers was few and far between, in that small city and so he too gained a notorious reputation for skilfully tackling the teething problems of electrically operated machines while they still had the capabilities to work on vintage machines that were built before they were born. There was no looking back for the world as mass-production and electricity – albeit from steam powered, coal fired plants, propelled economies to great heights! This was the way to go. But Grandpa was petrified of electricity and prayed for dad's safety. Accidents were not uncommon then. Technology and safety norms were still advancing. We often heard of innocent and un-schooled villagers and animals on farms being electrocuted due to lack of knowledge and awareness.

As I grew up to my teens, I was nurtured by dad – my hero, to love machines and technology and learned about the dangers and usefulness of electricity and just about anything that worked!

I soon graduated from my wooden tool kit to being trusted to play with his huge box of tools and by the age of 6, I knew how lights worked and the functions of all switches at home. This worked to a great advantage, and I was able to save my mother from being electrocuted when at that age! Her gold bangle accidentally touched a naked point on the ancient plug-in clothes iron that we had, and she was screaming while her body was being contorted backwards; she couldn't break loose either. I managed to turn off the right switch without panicking (as it was always drilled into me by dad). It took several months for her to recover as I remember. But that is the power of the right education at the right time.

From then on, holidays meant numerous trips to the ever-growing industrial estate and of course his first love, the textile mills. His dream and passion were that I should be an engineer as according to him, *there was nothing better for a man to do*! As I grew, all this fascinated me and then somehow, he motivated me to learn about electronics which was fast catching on. By the age of 10, with the help of a relative who was an ace in electronics and part of the design team for the railways' signalling and telecom systems, I learned about basic components and finally made my own two-band radio, among other little electronic gadgets, at 11 during the summer holidays. He was thrilled! By 15, after a short course in a radio institute, I could also strip a superheterodyne receiver (a three-band valve-based radio) and re-assemble it right from the component level.

Prologue

It was the 70s and the hippy age was in! The world was rapidly advancing, and India was not to be left behind! I final joined he Indian navy in the middle of 1979 and as far as technology was concerned, there was no looking back as I sailed through the 3rd industrial revolution and here I am, sharing my acquired knowledge of 4.0, in 2023!

For posterity's sake, here are some important events:

Date	Event
1712	**The steam engine is invented.** Thomas Newcomen invents the first steam engine. It is not very useful yet, but the idea of using steam to make machines go will be important to the Industrial Revolution.
1764	**The spinning jenny was invented.** James Hargreaves, a British carpenter and weaver, invents the spinning jenny. The machine spins more than one ball of yarn or thread at a time, making it easier and faster to make cloth.
1769	**James Watt improves the steam engine.** James Watt from Scotland designs a more efficient steam engine. One of the most important inventions of the Industrial Revolution, steam engines power the first trains, steamboats, and factories.
1794	**Eli Whitney patents the cotton gin.** Eli Whitney creates a machine that makes it much easier to separate cotton seeds from cotton fibre. It greatly reduces the time it takes to clean cotton and helps the southern states make more money from cotton crops.
1844	**Samuel Morse invents the telegraph.** Samuel Morse invents the telegraph, which allows messages to be sent quickly over a wire. By 1860, telegraph wires stretch from the east coast of the United States west of the Mississippi River.
1846	**Elias Howe invents the sewing machine.** At a time when people had to make their own clothes at home or pay someone else to sew them by hand, Elias Howe invents the sewing machine. Now clothes can be made in large factories.
1853	**Elisha Otis invents the elevator safety break.** Elevators were already invented by 1853, but people worried about elevator cars falling. Elisha Otis invents a safety break to prevent them from falling if a cable breaks, making people feel more confident about using elevators in tall buildings.
Jan 1855	**The Bessemer Method for processing steel is invented.**

Prologue

Date	Event
	Henry Bessemer invents a process for making steel out of iron. Having a way to make steel more quickly and more cheaply helps the production of building and leads to the growth of cities.
1866	**Alfred Nobel creates dynamite.** Alfred Nobel invents dynamite, which is a safer way to blast holes in mountains or the ground than simply lighting black powder. Dynamite is important in clearing paths to build things such as roads and railroad tracks.
Jan 1870	**Louis Pasteur develops vaccines for diseases.** A chemist named Louis Pasteur believed that germs caused disease. Using this information, he created vaccines that helped prevent many common diseases, which helped people live longer.
Mar 1876	**Alexander Graham Bell patents the telephone.** He may not have invented the telephone, but Alexander Graham Bell was the first to get a patent for it. Being able to speak to people over a telephone wire greatly changes the way the world communicates.
Oct 1879	**Thomas Edison uses a light bulb to light a lamp.** Not the first man to create a light bulb, Thomas Edison created a light bulb that lasted longer than other designs and showed it off by lighting a lamp. Edison's light bulbs allow people to do many things at night, such as work, that used to only happen during the day.
May 1883	**The Brooklyn Bridge opens.** After 13 years of construction, the Brooklyn Bridge is finished in New York City. At the time, it was the longest suspension bridge in the world.
Dec 1903	**Orville Wright makes the first powered airplane flight.** Using an engine that they invented, Orville and Wilbur Wright invent the first plane that is not powered by wind. Orville flies the plane for 12 seconds over a beach in North Carolina.
Oct 1908	**Henry Ford creates the Model T.** Henry Ford creates a type of car called the Model T. It is much cheaper than other cars because it is made on an assembly line, allowing many more people to buy cars.

Elstan A. Fernandez

Industry 4.0 for Maritime Operations and System Maintenance

★ The Industrial Revolutions

★ Emerging trends in the shipping industry

★ Current challenges in the maritime industry

★ Opportunities for innovation in the maritime industry

★ Introduction to Industry 4.0

★ Elements of Maritime 4.0

★ Cyber Physical Systems-based Predictive Maintenance

★ Impact of Industry 4.0 on the Maritime industry

★ Barriers of 4.0 Implementation

★ Drivers of 4.0 Implementation

★ Smart Ships

★ Emergence of new business models

9.1   The Industrial Revolutions

The History of mankind is full of innovations. In its quest to excel, mankind kept on inventing newer technologies for the welfare of the society. The Renaissance movement gave a tremendous boost to the modern industries. Traditional concepts of individual and family excellence slowly started turning into a collaborative effort leading to mass production. The focus slowly started shifting from the comfort of a household to a common work places.

Associated systems of Power, Water, Land utilisation, Health Care, Training and Development, Education, Markets etc evolved rapidly. This has given rise to colonies, urban centres, towns, and cities. However, at an early stage. As we know, necessity is the mother of all inventions, and so most innovations were through the display of determination, interest, passion, curiosity, and sometimes luck. The application of scientific knowledge and analysis was missing. The Principles of Scientific Management was published by Frederick Winslow Taylor who was famous for his methods to improve industrial efficiency. Parallelly, theses efforts gave rise to the Industrial Revolutions, which were well documented since the middle of the 18th Century and the 5th Industrial Revolution is around the corner! They are as follows:

1. Mechanization / Water Power, Coal, Mechanical Loom - 1765 - 84

2. Electricity, Assembly Systems, Conveyor System, Gas as a Fuel, Model T Ford - 1870

3. Electronics, Basic Automation, Computers, First PLC, Nuclear Energy - 1969

4. Internet Connectivity, Renewable Energy, People + Machine + Data – 2010.

Maritime 4.0 - The Future of Seafaring

9.2   Extract from an article by ABB.com

Quote

The need for smarter energy strategies will make it easier to introduce Industry 4.0 technologies.

The next ten years are a period of critical growth for the marine and shipbuilding sectors. Everybody is working flat-out to meet the demands of the market. At the same time, pressure is mounting on the industry to improve energy efficiency. Emissions reductions and cost reductions will be major drivers for Marine 4.0.

The International Maritime Organization (IMO) aims to reduce the average carbon intensity (CO2 emissions per transport work) by 40% in 2030 and 70% in 2050 compared to 2008 levels. The IMO also aims to reduce total GHG (Green House Gas) emissions from shipping by at least 50% in 2050 compared to 2008.

Analysis of Industry 4.0 investments by experts at McKinsey points to significant potential cost reductions. Industries that invest in digitalization could reduce their operational costs by 3.6% on average and improve efficiency by 4.1%. McKinsey also estimates that productivity increases of 3-5% are possible through investment in the Internet of Things, smart energy consumption, and remote monitoring and control. Predictive maintenance and virtually guided self-servicing could also reduce maintenance costs by 10% to 40%.

Unquote

These technologies are now being used in the retail sector, for telecom operations, e-governance, healthcare, logistics, supply chain, the shipping industry– in fact any vertical or horizontal which is integrating Data, Connectivity, which means any industry for that matter!

9.3	**Emerging Trends in The Shipping Industry**

- The use of alternatives to traditional fossil fuels e.g., solar, all-electric ships, hydrogen-based Fuel Cells as he main source of power

- Alternative fuel standards which are much higher in terms of being favourable to the environment.

- Increased automation of infrastructure (IIoT) leading to a massive reduction in manpower and higher quality standards.

- Seamless systems and process integration thereby increasing throughput and reducing downtime.

- Maritime Autonomous Surface Ships (MASS) are being tested and the concept vessels have far surpassed expectations after completing trans-oceanic voyages.

- Blockchain Technology, which is a shared, immutable ledger that facilitates the process of recording transactions and tracking assets in a business network. An asset can be tangible (a house, car, cash, land) or intangible (intellectual property, patents, copyrights, branding).

- 3D printing – reducing the following:

  - The need to transport basic components in bulk,

  - Lead times,

  - Financial loss as a whole

- Robotics has become an integral part of shipbuilding – especially where hazardous operations like welding of huge plates / sections are carried out, painting, lifting and transferring huge equipment from one section to another, and many other processes.

Legal and Regulatory Outlook

- Legal frameworks to improve monitoring of shipping containers by shore-based authorities has greatly reduced smuggling and transfer of illicit goods and other nefarious activities.

- Legal and health guidelines for transporting wildlife by air, land and sea is helping in the conservation of wildlife and preventing extinction too.

- Improved focus on ethics such as ensuring that unethically sourced raw materials do not enter the marketplace. These include materials like cobalt which are used for the manufacture of batteries for electronics and electric cars.

- Implementation of the Triple Bottom Line philosophy across the industry (People, Planet, Profit)

IMO 2020

- Improved standards on emission and carbon footprint by worldwide regulation authorities such as the IMO as well as local law enforcement agencies (see environmental challenges below)

9.4   Current Challenges in The Maritime Industry

Rising costs of fuel, lubricants and ship building has a ripple effect on trade and supply chain management. Cost of living for all increases in tandem.

Managing demand versus time versus more passengers. The world over, mankind is in a constant quest for faster and smarter ways to achieve stiffer targets and bigger goals in the least possible time.

Challenges in the Management of Operations

- The weather, although forecasted 24x7, always plays a major role in sea trade - communication during bad weather is difficult and expensive equipment is always needed. We therefore need scalable solutions and route control through quick communication and control to ensure safe passage of men and material.

- Information sharing is getting better as newer laws and better communication channels for information are opening. It is important that ships have updated and relevant documents and records that are maintained as stipulated in various regulations and safety management systems.

Environmental Challenges and Emissions

Global warming and climate change – so emissions are being cut down to a great extent. IMO 2020 is playing a great role in this regard. One example is that carbon emission is to be down by 50% by the year 2050.

Older and unsafe vessels must be de-commissioned, and the operating life span will come down. This will result in safer ships and a cleaner environment.

Many large ship building yards are proving that alternatives to HFO and Diesel Oil are Biofuels, Electricity, SOFCs and Solar, to name a few.

Digitization of Supply Chains

- Incompatibilities of systems, procedures, documentation and lack of knowledge are major hurdles for digitization. In short, it is the mindset that has to change if we have to adopt better technologies that are not as error prone as manual systems.

- Small scale operators lack the funds and expertise in most cases, as compared to large scale providers / operators being able to upgrade continuously and keep abreast with modern-day technologies. Very often, large scale operators are the agents of change.

- The burden as we see is lack of expertise in software, but we see the opportunity to create jobs for data scientists and technocrats in the shipping industry as they are already aware of universally accepted digital standards (like the internet and related software).

Changing Trade Patterns

- Changing trade tariffs due to policies and prices of critical commodities is a big challenge. Wars, changes in government and local leadership, stock markets and oil prices are a few influences.

Piracy – a menace that has been plaguing main shipping routes for decades.

Labour Shortages and changing workforce dynamics

- Labour upgrade to new tech and automation and robotics, VR and AR goggles onboard for operation, maintenance and repair based on new warranty versus guarantee, terms leading to replacement of whole systems due to design and lack of expertise onboard can impact the bottom line in financial statements.

Lack of funding and investments

- Gone are the days when individual investors and banks made impulsive investments in the shipping industry! Due to the volatility in the economy, many do not invest in a high-risk operation although the returns are very high. However, fortune favours the brave and that is the reason why the shipping industry is still ticking and contribution to about 90% of world trade.

Lack of transparency and traceability leading to drugs, weapons, narcotics, animals, stowaways, etc.

- Facilitate total transparency from farmer to shelf from factory to shelf

- Good Standard Operating Procedures are required for transport and traceability. Most companies do have very well-documented procedures and records that enhance traceability

9.5 Opportunities for Innovation in the Maritime Industry

Reduction Of Accidents

- 90% accidents due to human error and poor communication using radio waves hindered by poor weather

- Requirement of resilient communication systems with satellite communication

Digitization of Routing and Documentation for Cargo

Realtime Monitoring of Resources / Operational Status by Smart Sensors Installed

- Tracking delivery …now only at check pint or hub

- Use analytics to study behaviour

Better Info Sharing and Transparency

What happens when they are not ready to do so?

Innovation In Production and Manufacturing

Efficient Ship building

9.6   Introduction to Industry 4.0

It is essential to understand the potential of this fourth industrial revolution because it will affect manufacturing processes. Its range is much broader, involving all industries and sectors. Industry 4.0 can improve revenue growth, business operations, and transforms the supply chain, products, and customer expectations. Such a change will likely modify the way we do things.

Image courtesy: canva.com (from the author's subscribed account)

Technologies coupled to Industry 4.0 can lead to entirely new services and products. The use of portable devices and sensors, robotics, and analysis will allow improvements in products in numerous ways, from creating tests and prototypes to the integration of connectivity to previously disconnected products.

Now that we know the importance of industry 4.0 let's look at the core pillars of this technological revolution.

The 9 Pillars of Technological Advancements

Industry 4.0 is built on 9 technology pillars. These advancements bridge the digital and physical worlds and make autonomous and smart systems possible. Supply chains and businesses are already using some of these innovative technologies, but the full completion of Industry 4.0 comes at the front when used together.

1. Big Data and Analytics

2. Autonomous Robots

3. Industrial Internet of Things (IIoT)

4. Simulation / Digital Twin

5. Augmented Reality

6. Additive Manufacturing

7. Cybersecurity

8. Cloud Computing

9. Horizontal And Vertical System Integration

Industry 4.0 is all about sustainability to support the circular economy.

1. Big Data and Analytics

Analytics based on large data sets has come out recently in the world of manufacturing, where it optimizes quality of production, improves equipment service, and saves energy. It will become standard to support decision making in real-time. Big data and analytics are thus the use of advanced analytic techniques against very large, diverse big data sets that include structured, semi-structured and unstructured data, from different sources e.g., from production equipment, systems, and organizations. and in different, sizes from terabytes to zettabytes

Big Data enjoys a lot of hype and for a reason. But understanding the essence of Big Data and ways to analyse it is still blurred. The truth is, there's more to this term than just the amount of information generated. Not only does Big Data apply to the huge volumes of continuously growing data that come in different formats, but it also refers to the range of processes, tools, and approaches used to gain insights from that data. And that's the most important thing: Big Data analytics helps companies deal with business problems that couldn't be solved with the help of traditional approaches and tools.

To understand Big Data, you need to get acquainted with its attributes known as the four V's.

Volume is what's "big" in Big Data. This relates to terabytes to petabytes of information coming from a range of sources such as IoT devices, social media, text files, business transactions, etc.

Just so you can grasp the scale, 1 petabyte is equal to 1,000,000 gigabytes. A single HD movie on Netflix takes up over 4 gigabytes while you are watching. Now imagine that 1 petabyte contains 250,000 movies. And Big Data isn't about 1 petabyte, it's about thousands and millions of them.

Velocity is the speed at which the data is generated and processed. It's represented in terms of batch reporting, near real-time/real-time processing, and data streaming. The best-case scenario is when the speed with which the data is produced meets the speed with which it is processed. Let's take the transportation industry for example.

A single car connected to the Internet with a telematics device plugged in generates and transmits 25 gigabytes of data hourly at a near-constant velocity. And most of this data must be handled in real-time or near real-time.

Variety is the vector showing the diversity of Big Data. This data isn't just about structured data that resides within relational databases as rows and columns. It comes in all sorts of forms that differ from one application to another, and most of Big Data is unstructured. Say, a simple social media post may contain some text information, videos or images, a timestamp. etc.

Veracity is the measure of how truthful, accurate, and reliable data is and what value it brings. Data can be incomplete, inconsistent, or noisy, decreasing the accuracy of the analytics process. Due to this, data veracity is commonly classified as good, bad, and undefined. That's quite a help when dealing with diverse data sets such as medical records, in which any inconsistencies or ambiguities may have harmful effects.

2. Autonomous Robots

Manufacturers in numerous industries have used robots to tackle complex assignments, but now they're progressing towards greater utility. They are becoming more flexible, autonomous, and cooperative. And hence, they will interact and work safely with humans and learn from them. These robots and analytics chatbot will be economical and have a more excellent range of capabilities than those used in manufacturing today.

For example, Kuka, a European robotic equipment manufacturer, offers autonomous robots that interact. These robots are interconnected to work together and automatically adjust their actions to fit the next unfinished product in the line. Control units and High-end sensors enable close collaboration with humans.

Maritime 4.0 - The Future of Seafaring

Image courtesy: canva.com (from the author's subscribed account)

3. Internet of Things (IoT)

It is a computing concept which describes connecting everyday physical objects such as toasters and refrigerators, lights and other appliance to the internet and enabling them to communicate with each other.

Several factors such as high-speed network infrastructure and shared communication protocols – Machine to Machine (M2M) are needed for successful IoT implementation.

Industrial Internet of Things (IIoT)

In the current scenario, only some of a manufacturer's machines and sensors are networked and make use of embedded computing. The Industrial Internet of Things is so central to Industry 4.0 that the two terms are used interchangeably. Most of the physical things in Industry 4.0 – devices, machinery, robots, products, equipment, - use sensors to provide real-time data about their performance, condition, or location.

Image courtesy: canva.com (from the author's subscribed account)

This technology lets organizations run smoother supply chains, rapidly modify, and design products, stay on top of consumer preferences, prevent equipment downtime, track products and inventory, and much more.

Image courtesy: canva.com (from the author's subscribed account)

A drive-and-control-system vendor outfitted a production facility for valves with a decentralized production and semi-automated process. Products are identified by identification codes, radiofrequency, and workstations to know which manufacturing steps must be performed for each product and can adapt to perform the specific operation.

Internet of Services (IoS)

This is a global marketplace of internet-based software applications which is offered as "services".

IoS includes services such as Blockchain which is considered to be a game changer in the supply chain management space.

IoT facilitated by IoS creates disruptive innovation.

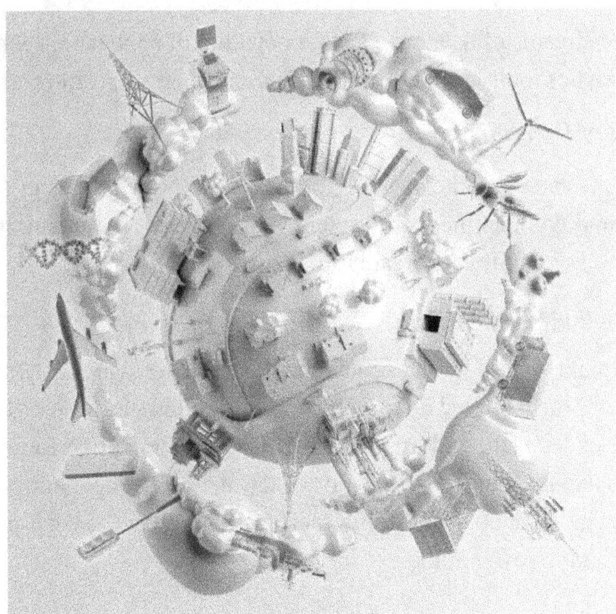

Image courtesy: canva.com (from the author's subscribed account)

Internet of People (IoP)

A radically new internet paradigm where humans and their personal devices are not considered as end users of applications but rather as active elements of the internet.

IoP runs on a de-centralised platform such as blockchain in which data and information is not stored or in control of a single entity.

IoP aims to be an internet for the people and of the people, rather than being one in which people unwittingly sacrifice their privacy.

Internet of Data (IoD)

It is built on the extensive data that is generated from the billions of IoT devices.

These streams of data have a huge potential of applications when Big Data analytics tools are used to identify trends in the streams of data.

Internet of Everything (IoE)

It is the integration of people, processes, data of things, in a single unified and complex network system. This includes extending the IoT, IIoT, IoS, IoP and IoD to create IoE

4. Simulation / Digital Twin

A digital twin is a virtual simulation of a real-world product, machine, system, or process based on IoT sensor data. It allows businesses to better analyse, understand, and improve the maintenance and performance of products and industrial systems. For instance, an asset operator can use a digital twin to identify a specific malfunctioning part, predict potential issues, and improve uptime.

A renowned international machine-tool vendor developed a virtual machine that can simulate the machining of parts utilizing the data from the physical machine. This shredded the setup time for the actual machining process by as much as 80 percent.

Virtual Reality is a fully digital, computer-generated, three-dimensional experiential environment. Unlike traditional user interfaces that only allow users to view a screen, VR allows the user to step inside an experience, to be immersed in and interact with a 3D world that can either simulate or differ completely from the real world. (Related: augmented reality medical training, VR medical training, AR + VR medical education)

By simulating the senses as possible – such as vision, hearing, and sometimes touch – a computer is transformed into a gatekeeper to a new world. The only limits to a VR experience are the availability of content and computing power.

There are 3 primary categories of virtual reality simulations used today: non-immersive, semi-immersive, and fully immersive simulations.

Non-Immersive Virtual Reality

Non-immersive virtual experiences are often overlooked as a virtual reality category because it's already so commonly used in everyday life. This technology provides a computer-generated environment but allows the user to stay aware of and keep control of their physical environment.

Non-immersive virtual reality systems rely on a computer or video game console, display, and input devices like keyboards, mice, and controller. A video game is a great example of a non-immersive VR experience.

Semi-Immersive Virtual Reality

Semi-immersive virtual experiences provide users with a partially virtual environment. It will still give users the perception of being in a different reality when they focus on the digital image, but also allows users to remain connected to their physical surroundings.

Semi-immersive technology provides realism through through 3D graphics, a term known as vertical reality depth. More detailed graphics result in a more immersive feeling. This category of VR is used often for educational or training purposes and relies on high-resolution displays, powerful computers, projectors, or hard simulators that partially replicate design and functionality of functional real-world mechanisms.

Fully Immersive Virtual Reality

Fully immersive simulations give users the most realistic simulation experience, complete with sight and sound. T

o experience and interact with fully immersive virtual reality, the user needs the proper VR glasses or a head mount display (HMD). VR headsets provide high-resolution content with a wide field of view.

The display typically splits between the user's eyes, creating a stereoscopic 3D effect, and combines with input tracking to establish an immersive, believable experience.

This type of VR has been commonly adapted for gaming and other entertainment purposes, but usage in other sectors, namely education, is increasing now as well. The possibilities for VR usage are endless.

Advantages of Virtual Reality Training

- ✓ Little/no risk.

- ✓ Safe, controlled area.

- ✓ Realistic scenarios.

- ✓ Can be done remotely saving time and money.

- ✓ Improves retention and recall.

- ✓ Simplifies complex problems/situations.

- ✓ Suitable for different learning styles.

- ✓ Innovative and enjoyable.

5. ***Augmented Reality (AR)*** is an enhanced version of the real physical world that is achieved by using digital visual elements, sound, or other sensory stimuli and delivered via technology. The added value of AR within ship construction areas allows for individuals to interact with virtual information in a physical environment (expanded details).

AR solutions help in the accomplishment of daily tasks by providing added details that improve employee's ability to interact with and diagnosis issues in a physical environment.

This technology has also demonstrated the ability to integrate with quality control measures where workers can evaluate work, with evaluations and corrections provided in real time.

What is the difference between VR & AR?

VR creates an immersive virtual environment, while AR augments a real-world scene. VR is 75 percent virtual, while AR is only 25 percent virtual.

VR requires a headset device, while AR does not. VR users move in a completely fictional world, while AR users are in contact with the real world.

AR incorporates three features: a combination of digital and physical worlds, interactions made in real time, and accurate 3D identification of virtual and real objects.

An augmented reality app (AR app) is a software application that integrates digital visual content (and sometimes audio and other types) into the user's real-world environment.

Mixed Reality is a blend of physical and digital worlds, unlocking natural and intuitive 3D human, computer, and environmental interactions. This new reality is based on advancements in computer vision, graphical processing, display technologies, input systems, and cloud computing.

Mixed reality is like augmented reality as it won't remove you from your surroundings, but rather read your surroundings and add digital objects to your environment.

However, unlike with AR content, which can be retrieved using a mobile device, you will need a headset to experience mixed reality.

6. *Additive* Manufacturing

It is the construction of 3D objects using a CAD model or a digital 3D model. 3D printing requires specialised materials which are either deposited, joined, or solidified layer by layer based on computer control.

Organizations have begun to adopt additive manufacturing mostly to produce individual components and prototypes.

Having Industry 4.0 in place, these additive-manufacturing methods will be widely used to make small batches of customized products that offer construction advantages, like high performance, lightweight designs, and more.

For example, aerospace organizations are using additive manufacturing to apply new designs that reduce aircraft weight and lower expenses for raw materials such as titanium.

7. *Cybersecurity*

Numerous organizations still rely on production systems and management, and that is disconnected or closed. With the use of standard communications protocols and increased connectivity with Industry 4.0, the need to protect manufacturing lines and critical industrial systems from cybersecurity threats increases drastically. As a result, reliable and secure communications and access management of machines and users are a must.

During the past year, various industrial equipment vendors have joined forces with cybersecurity companies through partnerships or acquisitions.

8. *Cloud* Computing

Cloud computing is the "great enabler" of digital transformation. In the present scenario, cloud technology goes way beyond scalability, speed, cost efficiencies, and storage.

It gives the foundation for most advanced technologies – from AI and ML to the IoT – and provides organizations with a way to organize. The data that power Industry 4.0 cloud computing technologies reside in the cyber-physical systems and cloud at the core of Industry 4.0 use the cloud to coordinate and communicate.

9. *Horizontal* And Vertical System Integration

Currently, most of the IT systems are not fully integrated. Organizations, customers, and suppliers are rarely closely linked. Functions in the organization are not fully integrated. From plants to products to automation—lacks complete integration.

But with Industry 4.0, organizations, functions, departments, and capabilities will become much more tenacious, as cross-organization, universal data-integration networks evolve and enable truly automated value chains.

Let's take an example; Boost Aerospace and Dassault Systems launched a collaboration platform that serves as a common workspace for manufacturing and design collaboration and is available as a service on a private cloud. It manages all the tricky tasks of exchanging product and production data among multiple partners.

9.7　Elements of Maritime 4.0

The maritime industry is in the process of developing collaborative platforms to improve the lifecycle of vessels that can leverage the connected capabilities of digital systems.

Facilitating the delivery of greater performance, lower ownership cost, increased safety and security, and reliability. However, to this point, there remains a lack of consolidated principles and characteristics for M4.0.

Maritime 4.0 refers to:

- The automated integration of real data into decision making.
- The adoption and implementation of connected technologies for design, production, and operation.
- Reduction of vessel environmental impact, related to production, operation, disposal (including emissions, underwater noise, and material utilization).
- Affordable and sustainable operation; and
- Reduction of risk, increasing safety and security.

Maritime 4.0 - The Future of Seafaring

These principles reflect the output of both interviews and literature. Where it was confirmed that there is not a comprehensive understanding for what intelligent vessels or 4.0 entails in respect to the maritime industry.

The desire for "M4.0" stems from the fact that we are embarking on the next phase of digitalization in the industry, both in reality and perception.

The four principles of M4.0 to be discussed are: (1) innovation, (2) sustainability, (3) safety and security, and (4) connected and automated operations.

Innovation: the integration, adoption, and inclusion of technology, that allows for and supports syncritic data.

Through consideration of the innovative data solutions, information relating to the vessel can be used to evaluate varying options and iterations for decision-making activities. When considering the necessary processes for data to be integrated from vessels across different elements of M4.0.

Sustainability: Designers, shipowners, and operators have in recent years requested the retrofitting of existing vessels and the development of new energy-efficient vessels with better performance and lower operating costs.

Sustainability therefore represents a mechanism that describes value considerations and can be reflected through either materials, noise generation, or other quantifiable matrices relating to sustainability.

The expectations and effects of this principal relates to the continued optimization need to meet the shipowner expectations to have rapidly modernized the fleet with the energy efficiency systems solutions on the ship.

Safety and Security: Determination of the appropriateness of data sources in relation to design parameters and application is critical to maintaining and delivering a reliable and safe vessel. The challenge for how to deliver this principle to the vessel requires consideration of how data is utilized and effectively integrated with other data sources.

Ensuring that the information being generated and collected is of paramount importance in order for proper decisions making taken. Failure to meet this can result in a negative value for those involved if the "context understanding" during data collections is unclear. Integrating and merging the data into viable and manageable virtual systems allows for 4.0 to deliver operational data protection that cannot be tampered or molested and improves upon the vessel as a system.

Connected and Automated Operation: through a desire for optimized vessels this principle refers to the actual level of digitalization and integration of the vessel. Leveraging data so that it can deliver the greatest value requires not only the information generated by the systems, but also recognition of the industrial business being served. This data-driven approach considers that under the current conditions there are many sensors that can be used to provide and generate many types of data.

The challenge therefore is not directly linked to this first stage, the challenge rather is in the ability to understand and develop new sensors and data streams that provide more value to the entire industry. Redundancy and modularity can be powerful together, because it allows a module to be taken away without the system losing a critical function of the vessel.

Some important aspects for consideration are as follows:

Vessel design which reflects the incorporation of data from existing and previous vessels for improvement and optimization of the vessel.

Vessel construction: The process of construction describes production process used to deliver the vessel to the customer, including consideration of the supply chain, manufacturing technologies, representing both time and money, incurred from design to delivery.

Operation: Marine transportation systems, diving operations, ports, dredging and waste disposal. Operation and usage are the actual conditions and behaviours of the vessel, generating and producing data used for decision making regarding navigation, fuel consumption and operating environment.

Service: Manufacturers, engineering consultant firms in marine electronics and instrumentation, machinery, tele-communications, navigation systems, special-purpose soft-ware and decision support tools, research and exploration, and environmental monitoring.

The objective of M4.0 is for the delivery of a high-quality, optimized, and reliable vessel that leverages the latest technologies for the maximisation of customer value.

9.8   Cyber Physical Systems-based Predictive Maintenance

Industry 4.0 is the current trend of CPS which comprises of smart machines, storage systems and production facilities which have the capabilities of autonomously exchanging in formation, triggering actions, and controlling each other without little or no human intervention

This facilitates exponential improvements in manufacturing, engineering, resource usage, supply chain and product life cycle management

Cyber Physical systems are systems that will link the physical world using sensors and controllers with the digital (cyber) world

CPS is an integration of computing manpower, networking, and physical representation of a physical process or entity

The main purpose of CPS is to control a physical process and through continuous feedback, self-adapt and self-optimise itself in real time

CPS has become the key infrastructure in supporting the development of smart manufacturing in Industry 4.0

Advantages of CPS

- ✓ Integration

- ✓ Interaction between humans and CPS

- ✓ Managing uncertainty

- ✓ Better system performance

- ✓ Scalability

- ✓ Agility and flexibility

- ✓ Faster response time

Highlights of the EWS Project submitted by Vikas Dhawan and Elstan A. Fernandez for the AGORIZE Big Idea Challenge in Singapore in 2019. Hopefully, this will stimulate others to work towards better solutions too!

We will use IIOT to allow the various support agencies in the industry to connect in different geographies and time-zones to:

- Monitor plant performance from remote locations, and view all critical parameters through visual dashboards, in Real-Time.

- Enable Condition-based monitoring (CBM), and reduce expensive downtime, give warning of safety issues, and continuously monitor the health of machines

- Use remote cloud-based monitoring of installations to enable a high level of integration with customers.

Manage the over-whelming data overload. Unlock greater value through Data and Connectivity. Integrate all Data to a common platform:

- Connect Data from all machines and auxiliary equipment to an ERP system; access a Management Console for reports and analytics; download customized advanced reports on every ship.

- Tag, Process and Store of all Data assets as well as of the millions of Data points coming in every day from the machines and other digitalized systems of the fleet. Also sort and back-up all this data securely on the Cloud

- Use Analytics to make sense of the Data to predict customer needs in advance, trigger timely interventions, augment human capabilities, and control Process efficiencies

- Big data Analytics Services

- Data Security

The First step will be Predictive Maintenance:

This is done through Condition-based Monitoring and will have the following advantages:

- Maximize Revenues

- Reduce expensive down-time

- Synchronize maintenance with scheduled down-time

- Reduce total cost of Maintenance

- Eliminate secondary damages due to catastrophic breakdowns

- Perform tasks only when warranted

- Maximize Safety, reduce accidents

- Use Data Analytics to anticipate issues with each system

9.9 Impact of Industry 4.0 on the Maritime industry

1. Cyber Physical System-based operations

2. Cyber Physical System -based Predictive Maintenance

3. Cloud Computing

4. Computer simulations of Maritime Industry Ops

5. Robotics and Automation

6. Virtual Reality and Augmented Reality

7. Big Data Analytics

8. Distributed ledger technology and transparency

9. Automation of processes via bots

10. Autonomous Ships and barges

1. *CPS-based Operations*

There are 2 types of logistics in the manufacturing process namely production logistics and outbound logistics

Optimisation of production logistics has several benefits – resource utilisation enhancement, reduced product lead times, reduced manufacturing inventory, reduced costs, flexibility in internal manufacturing and logistics processes, increased product quality and integration of production logistics with enterprise resource planning (ERP) such as SAP

2. *CPS-based Predictive Maintenance*

Corrective Maintenance	Preventive Maintenance	Predictive Maintenance
Replacement after a breakdown	Increases asset lifespan	Holistic asset visibility
Leads to unplanned downtime	Cost effective	Cost effective
High maintenance costs	Saves energy and resources	Able to predict when failure will occur
Aimed at restoring an asset to a condition in which it can perform its intended function	Efficient productivity	Increases asset life cycle
	Reduces unplanned downtime	Downtime only before unavoidable circumstances

CPS-based components enable asset owners to make dynamic adjustments of maintenance activities while considering the risks and costs associated with it

✓ Using data mining techniques from CPS data, predictive algorithms can predict which component is likely to fail and when.

✓ Support the maintenance personnel by easily identifying components which are most likely to fail.

✓ Due to this real-time monitoring of components, a continuous improvement of operations is possible.

✓ Increased availability of assets and reduced unplanned downtime.

✓ Creates opportunities for new business models (Maintenance as Service MaaS)

3. *Cloud* Computing Services

- Cloud computing is the on-demand availability of computing resources such as data storage, databases, and computing power without direct active management by the end user.

- Cloud computing offers its services in terms of:

  - Software-as-a-Service (SaaS) – applications are provided in the cloud.

  - Platform-as-a-Service (PaaS) – users can run or deploy apps on the underlying services, with the operating systems being provided by the service provider.

  - Infrastructure-as-a-Service – an end user can deploy a computing infrastructure similar to a virtual environment.

- Cloud computing services will enable the Maritime Industry to deploy Artificial Intelligence (AI) and machine Learning (ML) solutions.

- Availability of e-Services such as tracking and tracing of shipments in real time, booking, freight rate compensation, routing, and scheduling of shipments, etc.

- Portals which connect suppliers, customers and manufacturers on a single platform enable a higher level of information being shared, resulting in tangible benefits such as more efficient business operations, etc.

- Streamlining of expenses incurred due to imports and custom processes.

- Reducing transportation costs by using Big Data Analytics and helping businesses to make better decisions.

- Meeting regulatory compliance with the use of intelligence software agents who report to regulatory agencies about any beyond tolerance metrics.

4. *Computer* Simulation of Maritime Industry Operations

- Ship and boat manufacturers can gain a lot of benefits from using computer simulation software in their design processes.

- Computer simulations can help to reduce hydrodynamic drag by using data rather real-life testing and assumptions.

- CPS systems can assist operators in predicting which components are most likely to fail and which components highly susceptible to wear and tear.

  This data can be directly fed into computer simulations to make future designs better as well as improve the current vessels.

- Computer simulations will also enable manufacturers to lower the centre of gravity to reduce the possibility of vessels capsizing.

5. *Robotics and Automation*

- Automation versus Autonomation – Automation is the use of machines, intelligent systems, and processes to do repeatable and mundane tasks without human intervention. Autonomation is automation with a human touch (the machine stops when an anomaly is detected, and humans can assist to fix it)

- Challenges in the maritime manufacturing industry such as non-standardised components, extremely heavy parts, complex geometrics of components, non-standard – one-of-a-kind tasks, processes and systems are however making the application of robotics quite difficult.

- With the increase of AI components such as computer vision and object recognition, robots will get smarter with time. Real-time object detection algorithms will continue to learn and thus reinforce the lessons to other applications such as picking objects, welding, handling containers, etc.

6. BDA in the Maritime Industry

Operations

- ✓ Maximise energy savings during operations.
- ✓ Safely guiding vessels along routes
- ✓ Schedule management
- ✓ Usage of dashboards to monitor information in real time.
- ✓ Reduce bunkering costs.

Technical Management of the vessel

- ✓ Safe operation of the vessel
- ✓ Real-time monitoring of the vessel's condition and maintenance activities
- ✓ Environmental protection regulations and governance
- ✓ Cleaning of components of the vessel such as the hull and propellers from barnacles, etc.

New Vessel Building

Design optimisation and improved hydrodynamics

Chartering

- ✓ Chartering involves finding the best value for money to deliver the cargo.

✓ BDA can assist in aggregation of information from a variety of sources such as Automatic Identification System (AIS), vessel characteristics such as maximum loading capacity, size, etc and other market insights on a single platform.

✓ Find alternatives if necessary.

Ports and related authorities

✓ Cargo handling operation / streamlining of the movement of goods.

✓ Timely maintenance of machinery such as cranes within the port

✓ Integrating services such as weather to better safety and health concerns

✓ Better analysis of reefer containers for any potential or harmful health hazards

Challenges in implementing BDA in the Maritime Industry

Increasing Cyber Threats

✗ CPS and other cyber equipment are vulnerable to ever-increasing cyber-attacks.

✗ Poor cyber security expertise within the maritime and related entities

Inaccurate data generated by maritime entities.

Broadcasting fake call signs, inaccurately mentioning the next port of call, etc., will result in extremely incorrect analysis of information and lead to poor decision-making by the industry.

Other challenges in the industry taking precedence over BDA apps

Challenges such as labour shortages, over-supply and market fluctuation take precedence over BDA applications in the industry.

Lack of shared technology implementation

Companies are focused on their functional silos rather than viewing the holistic picture and improving the entire maritime industry by using technological solutions.

Lack of skills / expertise

There is a dearth of data scientists to build BDA solutions.

7. *Distributed Ledger Technology and Transparency*

DLT is a de-centralised digital database of an auditable and immutable (unchanging) nature.

Once information is altered, it is shared with all the nodes in the network, and it does not have a controlling / governing entity.

A Smart Contract is a self-executing code which executes once a set of pre-determined conditions are satisfied like a contract. Smart Contracts can be used to check conditions when selling a ship, unloading cargo, etc.

Assistance in reducing crime and fraud as traceability will help the regulatory bodies to identify and punish the relevant entities and personnel.

It ensures that the health and safety standards for perishable items such as food in reefer containers are up to international standards.

8. *Automation Of Processes Via Bots*

Usage of Robotic Process Automation to automate repetitive and mundane tasks

Robotic process automation is a form of business process automation technology based on software robots or on artificial intelligence / digital workers. It is also known as software robotics or bots.

It offers up to about 70% in cost reduction and 3x faster processing

Pre-automation implementation will require evaluation of all processes and standardising all the inputs, outputs, and the processes too. This will further enhance the efficiency of processes within the industry.

Bots can be used for a variety of tasks such as:

- Crew clearance – preparing the immigration and emigration documents.

- Inform ports and harbours about the arrivals and departures of vessels.

- Reading standard operating procedures of the industry

- Better compliance and governance within the industry to reduce fraud, malpractices, and corruption.

- Scheduling and tracking of shipments.

- Processing of invoices and collecting credit from vendors

- Monitoring and ensuring the maximum safe loads are carried in vessels

- Automated processing of shipping orders and shipment

- Automated email notifications to each stakeholder about the payments (when arrived / picked-up, etc)

- Automated processing of procurement and inventory management (etc ordering when minimum order quantity has been reached)

- Faster invoicing due to seamless integration between different portals of different entities

- Faster processing of claims and customer queries

9. *Autonomous* Ships and Barges

Level of automation – degree three – remotely controlled vessels with no personnel on board

Level of automation –degree four – fully autonomous vessel which can analyse its environment and make decisions on its own.

9.10   Barriers of 4.0 Implementation

- ✗ High cost of Implementation
- ✗ Privacy issues and related concerns
- ✗ Lack of skilled staff
- ✗ Tech integration
- ✗ Lack of standardisation and co-ordination across industries

9.11   Drivers of 4.0 Implementation

1. Faster time to market
2. Challenges in matching supply and demand
3. Better Customer Experience
4. Increasing efficiency and productivity in business processes
5. Demand for better quality
6. Tech-augmented work force
7. The digital and agile supply chain
8. Better asset utilisation

Maritime 4.0 - The Future of Seafaring

1. Faster Time to Market

- Time to market (TTM) is the length of time from a product being conceived to the product being available for sale.

- Being late erodes the addressable market that you must sell your product into.

- Factors that can enable faster time to market are concurrent / simultaneous engineering and not traditional engineering. Both are explained in the two figures that follow.

Traditional Engineering

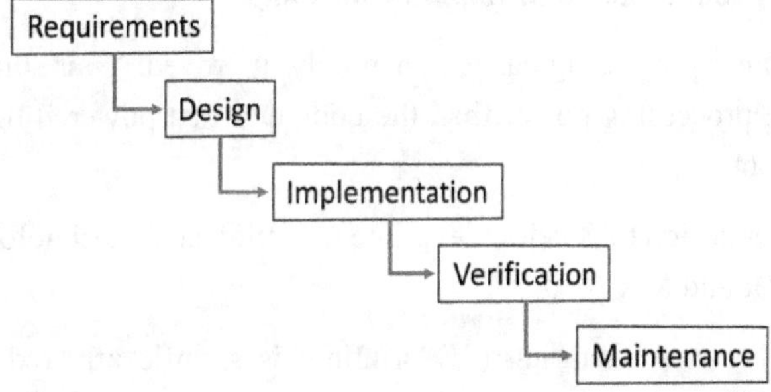

Simultaneous Engineering

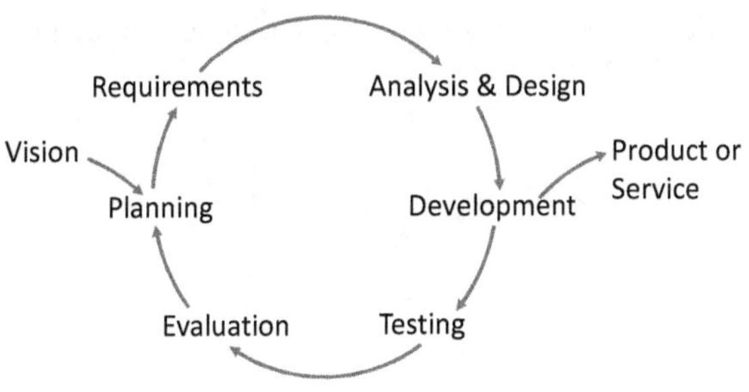

Advantages Of Concurrent / Simultaneous Engineering

- ✓ Various tasks are done simultaneously.

- ✓ Small inventory and fast turnover

- ✓ Multi-skilled staff who take on multiple projects and are flexible.

- ✓ Continuous / daily improvements are made.

- ✓ Promotes collaboration.

- ✓ Continuous upskilling of people

- ✓ Production is driven by a "pull" system based on customer orders.

Computer Simulation and Rapid Prototyping

Computer processing has exponentially improved. Your smart phone has more processing power than the computer that powered the Apollo 11 program.

Greater design to development time reduction using technologies such as AR, VR and MR

Additive manufacturing (3D printing) is significantly reducing the time taken to make prototypes.

Sharing of virtual prototypes which are built using tools such as AutoCAD, are further improving the design to development process.

Maritime 4.0 - The Future of Seafaring

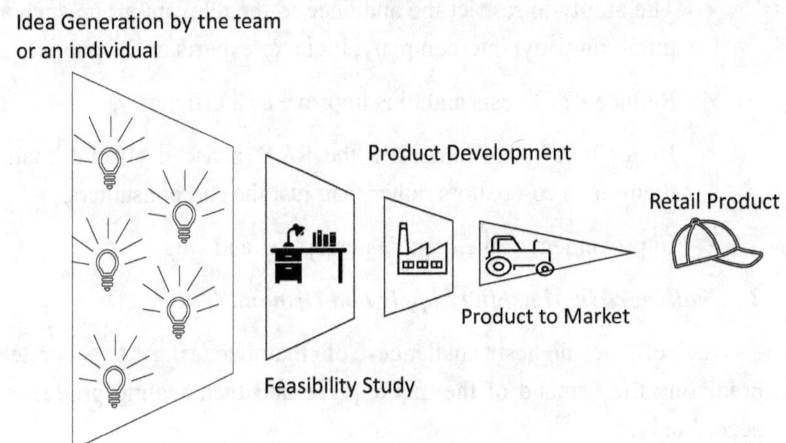

Closed (Traditional) Innovation

Open Innovation and Product Co-creation

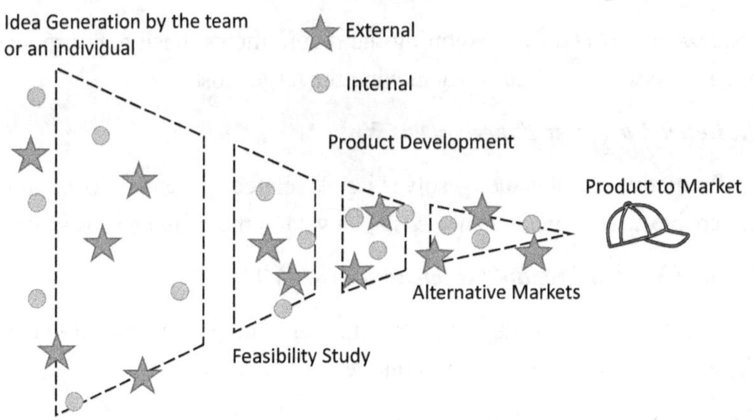

Benefits of Open Innovation

✓ The ability to engage with a larger audience for R&D activities rather than the usual R&D dept personnel.

- ✓ The ability to restrict the audience to the relevant group such as intra-company, intercompany, industry experts or the public.

- ✓ Reduce R&D costs and thus improve cost efficiency.

- ✓ Better involve customers in the R&D phase itself and enable them to be co-creators rather than just the end consumers.

- ✓ Improvement of the brand's perception and value

2. *Challenges In Matching Supply and Demand*

One of the biggest challenges of manufacturing is accurately predicting the demand of the marketplace and then scaling production accordingly.

Design-to-value (DTV) – capturing the requirements; designing products and services which focuses on maximising the value delivered to the customer

Design-to-cost (DTC) – capturing the requirements; designing products and services which focus on achieving the target cost

3. *Better Customer Experience (CX)*

Predictive maintenance – solves issues related to business continuity, expensive ad hoc maintenance costs, unwanted maintenance costs, etc.

Remote Monitoring and Maintenance (RMM)

Remotely monitoring and maintaining smart devices. Remotely deploying upgrades and updates online.

Robots / Self-Service Robots / Chatbots

Virtual robots who act as customer support agents, self-guided tutorials and tools, automation.

4. *Increasing Efficiency and Productivity in Business Processes*

✓ *Smart energy consumption*

✓ Smart logistics – better real-time monitoring of the supply chain with end-to-end monitoring – e.g., smart pallets

✓ Cyber physical systems / self-aware robots which are capable of self-organising, self-optimising, and self-learning without or with minimum human supervision.

5. *Demand For Better Quality*

Statistical Quality Control

- Usage of stats to monitor and control a process. Massive amount of data can be extracted using IoT, CPS, and IIoT devices as well as other sources to improve the quality management process.

- Automation / robots

- Using automation and robots in the production lines to improve the quality of products.

Advanced Process Control

APC is added on top of basic process control to address performance issues or economic improvement opportunities in the process.

Digital Quality Management (DQM)

Digital tools to improve and monitor quality issues such as errors, inconsistencies, etc.

6. Tech-augmented Worker

Human Computer Interaction (HCI)

Designing computer systems which focus on creating and engaging user experience.

Human Robot Collaboration

Workers and robots working together to achieve a shared goal.

Remote monitoring and control

Remotely monitoring equipment and over-the-air updates and upgrades

Digital Performance Management

Monitoring of the performance and productivity of digital transactions and appliances

Knowledge Automation

Use technologies such as Machine learning to fix knowledge gaps in business.

7. The Digital and Agile Supply Chain

On-site 3D Printing

3D printing of spares on-site to reduce production and service disruptions, reduce cost, etc

Real-time Supply Chain Optimisation

Route optimisation, better risk mitigation, crisis management, etc

Real-time Yield Optimisation

Right place, right time, right price, and right quantity

9.12 Case Studies

An example of a case study (courtesy www.maindeck.io)

Problem

Simplifying costly, complex ship repairing and maintenance for ship owners; comprehensive cloud-based management suite to reduce unforeseen cost and delays.

Solution

- ✓ Software as a Service (SaaS)
- ✓ Specify focus on dry-docking projects.
- ✓ Standard work orders, smart suggestion on projects
- ✓ Comparison of yards, progress updates reports, understand dependencies.
- ✓ Fleet dashboard, application program interface for easy connectivity

An example a case study (courtesy www.nautixtech.com)

Problem

Improving the safety, efficiency, and reliability of shipping ops

Solution

- ✓ Cloud-based solution for operations scheduling on ship and shore
- ✓ Real-time tracking and collaboration
- ✓ Task assignment, risk assessment, permission to work, reporting, operations-based performance rating, setting of operational benchmarks.

An example a case study (courtesy www.iocurrents.com)

Problem

Increasing the uptime and efficiency using Big Data Analytics platform

Solution

- ✓ Analyses everything onboard and creates a real-time data twin.

- ✓ Machine learning models to detect anomalies and alert crew.

- ✓ Smart gauges enable operators to view the conditions of reefer containers in real time to ensure quality standards are met.

An example a case study (courtesy www.arviem.com)

Problem

Supply chain visibility is only possible at checkpoints.

Solution

- ✓ IoT-enabled end-to-end real-time supply chain visibility solution.

- ✓ Strict monitoring of temperature, humidity, shock, and intrusion alerts via email

- ✓ Business intelligence with Big Data for better ETA

- ✓ Pay only for what you use.

9.13   Smart Ships

Extract from an online article by Bureau Veritas

Quote

Why develop smart ships?

Smart ships offer many benefits to ship owners and operators. Advanced sensor technology, data analytics and connectivity support onboard and remote monitoring and decision support systems for machinery and navigation equipment.

The integration of smart equipment enables operators to improve operational performance and efficiency, while reducing emissions, optimizing maintenance and controlling operating costs.

Navigational aids improve safety by limiting collision and grounding risk, and support the development of autonomous navigation systems, which will further reduce reliance on crew.

What are the main challenges for developing smart ships?

For equipment and systems manufacturers, the key question is how to achieve certification in an unregulated area of technological development. System functionality and reliability, cyber security and data protection, product liability, onboard and onshore equipment integration and more must be considered.

Ship owners and operators are confronted by questions of high CAPEX and uncertainty as they choose among competing technologies. Meanwhile, classification societies and regulatory bodies need to develop standards, regulations, and guidelines for all aspects of smart shipping, from equipment certification, to design assessment, to cyber security.

Do regulations currently exist for smart ships?

In 2006, IACS published UR E22, the first in a series of unified requirements addressing cyber resilience and the interplay among ship systems.

The 2016 revision of these requirements includes specific testing standards for software certification and the integration of onboard equipment. In April 2020, the IACS Cyber Panel – chaired by Bureau Veritas' Vincent Lagny – further published a standalone recommendation for Cyber Resilience, REC N° 166.

IMO has also released interim guidelines for autonomous ship trials, as well as guidelines to standardize user interfaces and data exchanged by e-navigation systems. An ISO working group for smart shipping is also developing general, standardized terminology for Maritime Autonomous Surface Ships (MASS).

At Bureau Veritas, we have issued Guidelines for Autonomous Shipping (NI 641), a Rules Note on Cyber Security (NR 659) and an additional service feature for smart ships in our updated NR 467 Rules for Steel Ships.

What asset types are suited to smart shipping?

Although all ships can theoretically be automated, there is a strong business case for automating already-connected and tech-enabled vessels. These include passenger ships, ships carrying sensitive cargo (e.g., LNG carriers), research vessels and offshore construction support vessels (which often have Dynamic Positioning systems). Inland navigation vessels are also interesting candidates for smart shipping, thanks to easy connectivity and well-defined routing.

Maritime 4.0 - The Future of Seafaring

As smart technology advances, different asset types will see varying levels of onboard integration based on individual needs. There is no one-size-fits-all model for smart shipping, and ship technologies may range from smart machinery to fully autonomous navigation systems.

What expertise will marine actors need to develop to achieve smart shipping?

Smart shipping will require flag states, classification societies, ship owners, equipment manufacturers and shipyards to develop standards for assessing the safety, reliability, and functionality of automated and integrated systems. This means improving systems engineering and cybernetics skills, as computer scientists develop new human-machine interfaces and machine learning technologies.

These developments will help ships and systems recognize patterns, provide suggestions, and ultimately make and execute decisions. From a classification perspective, plan approval engineers and ship surveyors will need to learn new inspection techniques and standards. This will allow them to evaluate ship design and certify connected onboard systems and equipment using advanced testing and simulation techniques.

Unquote

Extract from an article by ABB.com

Quote

The Marine Innovation Challenges

The case for Industry 4.0 may be well established; but plans for Marine 4.0 and Shipbuilding 4.0 are less advanced. For organizations already using high levels of automation, Industry 4.0 and digitalization of operations can be a relatively small step.

In sectors where investments are larger and their life cycles significantly longer and more challenging, it's a different story.

Innovation in marine engineering and shipbuilding is not like other sectors. The unique challenges that face operations at sea mean there will be significant differences. The digitalization strategies and the type of technical partnerships will be different because the barriers to adoption are greater.

It is not just that any solution must survive the demands of a working life at sea. The opportunities for innovative solutions to enter the product life cycle are fewer and the timescales tighter.

In some cases, when shipbuilders produce new models, they then spend several years simply replicating their initial design. The moment for innovation is often limited to the first prototype. Stretched-for-time engineering departments often need more specialist technical support and more collaborative partnerships with suppliers, particularly for digital solutions that are not part of the core engineering resources.

There are lessons to be learned from other sectors, however. The way building management, for example, has benefited from Industry 4.0 and IoT advances shows how small advances can have a significant impact.

Thinking small to advance

With data-gathering and networking, smart buildings can monitor costs and consumption for individual rooms.

A thousand-passenger cruise ship requires a power generation system on the order of 50 megawatts — enough to supply a town of 50,000 inhabitants. This requires high levels of granularity for the metering to understand the impact on the ship's overall fuel consumption.

Maritime 4.0 - The Future of Seafaring

In merchant ships, although it is obvious that refrigerated containers cost more to ship than other containers since they draw a lot of energy, in practice, the costs are distributed uniformly across all the containers onboard. With the right distributed metering and connectivity onboard, a reefer ship will be able to determine its energy demands and allocate its costs more accurately. Better cargo tariffs could be defined for different routes, charging a premium, for example, for travel near the equator where cooling costs are higher.

The focus so far has been on the bigger challenges, but attitudes are changing. In naval circles, the energy systems on board a ship are increasingly considered to be mission critical. Some marine operators and shipbuilders are also looking further down the chain for Industry 4.0 opportunities in electrification and low-voltage power. In the face of the emissions challenge, every major operator must renovate their fleet; many have decided that retrofitting existing fleets is the best strategy.

We know the concept of smart electrical distribution based on smart devices with connectivity is an area many would like to explore more. We believe it is a good place to start. We have retrofit solutions that make it simpler to trial and an innovation centre where we work directly with customers to quickly develop –- and validate –- solutions that are right for their vessels. For any company looking for support in Marine 4.0 electrification, our door is open.

Unquote

9.14   Emergence of New Business Models

Sharing Economy Business Models

Low CAPEX cost, convenience, and experience at a fraction of the Total Cost of Ownership (TCO)

Personalisation Economy Business Models

Products which are curated by experts, tailored, and customised according to an individual customer's tastes and preferences.

Replenishment Economy Business Models

Smart sensors such as IoT detect low quantities of products and automatically re-order them and deliver them to the customer.

X as a Service

Anything as a service – providing flexibility of seamlessly scaling up, scaling down, diversifying the business, ability to focus on the core business rather than fire-fighting other issues. The benefits include financial efficiencies and affordability of world-class services by SMEs. However, (SMEs also run the risk of being exploited by such agencies.

9.15   The Future

The Universal Robots chief technology officer and co-founder, explained, "Industry 5.0 will make the factory a place where creative people can come and work, to create a more personalized and human experience for workers and their customers." By connecting how machine and man work together, estimates say that Industry 5.0 will mean that over 60% of manufacturing, logistics and supply chains, agri-farming, and the mining and oil and gas sectors will employ chief robotics officers by 2025.

Note*: information for the 9 pillars of 4.0 and the future also includes reference to info available on the website* *https://www.polestarllp.com/*

***

For Books on following Subjects

- Business, Management & Finance
- Career Development, Career Guides
- Catering & Hotel Management / Recipes
- Civil Engineering
- Computers
- Communication
- Dental / Health / Medical
- Economics
- Electrical Engineering
- Electronics & Communication
- English
- Entrepreneurship
- Environmental Engineering
- Event Management
- Fiction
- Forensic Science
- General Titles
- HRD
- International Trade
- Law
- Learning Disability
- Mathematics
- Mechanical Engineering
- Media
- Mobile Computing
- Motivation & Self Help
- Parenting
- Patent
- Physics
- Project Management / Software Engineering
- Real Estate
- Statistics

Publishers We Represent